Applying the Standards: STEM
Grade 3

Credits
Content Editors: Elise Craver, Natalie Rompella

Visit *carsondellosa.com* for correlations to Common Core, state, national, and Canadian provincial standards.

Carson-Dellosa Publishing, LLC
PO Box 35665
Greensboro, NC 27425 USA
carsondellosa.com

ISBN 978-1-4838-1574-9
01-005151151

Table of Contents

Introduction

STEM education is a growing force in today's classroom. Exposure to science, technology, engineering, and math is important in twenty-first century learning as it allows students to succeed in higher education as well as a variety of careers.

While it can come in many forms, STEM education is most often presented as an engaging task that asks students to solve a problem. Additionally, creativity, collaboration, communication, and critical thinking are integral to every task. STEM projects are authentic learning tasks that guide students to address a variety of science and math standards. Also, students strengthen English Language Arts skills by recording notes and written reflections throughout the process.

In this book, students are asked to complete a range of tasks with limited resources. Materials for each task are limited to common household objects. Students are guided through each task by the steps of the engineering design process to provide a framework through which students can grow their comfort level and independently complete tasks.

Use the included rubric to guide assessment of student responses and further plan any necessary remediation. Confidence in STEM tasks will help students succeed in their school years and beyond.

Student Roles

Student collaboration is an important component of STEM learning. Encourage collaboration by having students complete tasks in groups. Teach students to communicate openly, support each other, and respect the contributions of all members. Keep in mind that collaborative grouping across achievement levels can provide benefits for all students as they pool various perspectives and experiences toward a group goal.

Consider assigning formal roles to students in each group. This will simplify the collaborative tasks needed to get a project done and done well. The basic roles of group structure are as follows:

- The *captain* leads and guides other students in their roles.

- The *guide* walks the team through the steps, keeps track of time, and encourages the team to try again.

- The *materials manager* gathers, organizes, and guides the use of materials.

- The *reporter* records the team's thoughts and reports on the final project to the class.

STEM Performance Rubric

Use this rubric as a guide for assessing students' project management skills. It can also be offered to students as a tool to show your expectations and scoring. Note: Some items may not apply to each project.

4	_____ Asks or identifies comprehensive high-level questions
	_____ Makes valid, nontrivial inferences based on evidence in the text
	_____ Uses an appropriate, complete strategy to solve the problem
	_____ Skillfully justifies the solution and strategy used
	_____ Offers insightful reasoning and strong evidence of critical thinking
	_____ Collaborates with others in each stage of the process
	_____ Effectively evaluates and organizes information and outcomes
3	_____ Asks or identifies ample high-level questions
	_____ Exhibits effective imagination and creativity
	_____ Uses an appropriate but incomplete strategy to solve the problem
	_____ Justifies answer and strategy used
	_____ Offers sufficient reasoning and evidence of critical thinking
	_____ Collaborates with others in most stages of the process
	_____ Evaluates and organizes some information or outcomes
2	_____ Asks or identifies a few related questions
	_____ Exhibits little imagination and creativity
	_____ Uses an inappropriate or unclear strategy for solving the problem
	_____ Attempts to justify answers and strategy used
	_____ Demonstrates some evidence of critical thinking
	_____ Collaborates with others if prompted
	_____ Evaluates and organizes simple information and outcomes
1	_____ Is unable to ask or identify pertinent questions
	_____ Does not exhibit adequate imagination and creativity
	_____ Uses no strategy or plan for solving the problem
	_____ Does not or cannot justify answer or strategy used
	_____ Demonstrates limited or no evidence of critical thinking
	_____ Does not collaborate with others
	_____ Cannot evaluate or organize information or outcomes

Name _____

Read the task. Then, follow the steps to complete the task.

Float Your Boat

Use only the aluminum foil provided to create a boat that can hold the most marbles without sinking.

Materials

1-foot (30 cm)-square piece of aluminum foil
water container, water

marbles (or a variety of objects to weigh, such as dice, counters, or eraser caps)

Ask

What do you already know? What do you need to know to get started? Where can you find the information you need?

_____

_____

_____

Imagine

What are the possibilities? Come up with several different options.

_____

_____

Plan

Choose an idea. Draw a model and label it. Consider making different models for each stage of construction or separate diagrams of more complex parts.

📓 Plan

What are your steps? Use your drawing to guide your plan. Number your steps and write clearly so that others can understand them.

_____

_____

_____

_____

🛠️ Create

Follow your plan to create your model. What worked? What didn't? What did you need to change as you went through your plan? Why?

_____

_____

_____

🔄 Improve

How could you improve your model? Do you need to start over, or can you redo a single part? If it works, can it work even better?

_____

_____

_____

💬 Communicate

How well did it work? Is the problem solved? Write a statement to describe how your model meets the guidelines of the task and why it is successful.

_____

_____

_____

☀️ Reflect

How did the shape of the boat affect its strength?

_____

_____

_____

_____

Name _____

Read the task. Then, follow the steps to complete the task.

Happily Hidden: Camouflage

Create a habitat and a creature that is camouflaged from view.

Materials

art supplies, such as
   markers or crayons
chenille stems
construction paper
cotton balls
craft sticks

glue
scissors
shoe box
small rocks
sticks and twigs
tape

Caution: Before beginning any nature activity, ask families' permission and inquire about students' plant and animal allergies. Remind students not to touch plants or animals during the activity.

Ask

What do you already know? What do you need to know to get started? Where can you find the information you need?

_____

_____

_____

Imagine

What are the possibilities? Come up with several different options.

_____

_____

_____

Plan

Choose an idea. Draw a model and label it. Consider making different models for each stage of construction or separate diagrams of more complex parts.

📝 Plan

What are your steps? Use your drawing to guide your plan. Number your steps and write clearly so that others can understand them.

_____

_____

_____

_____

🛠️ Create

Follow your plan to create your model. What worked? What didn't? What did you need to change as you went through your plan? Why?

_____

_____

_____

🔄 Improve

How could you improve your model? Do you need to start over, or can you redo a single part? If it works, can it work even better?

_____

_____

_____

💬 Communicate

How well did it work? Is the problem solved? Write a statement to describe how your model meets the guidelines of the task and why it is successful.

_____

_____

_____

☀️ Reflect

Does your creature's camouflage keep it safe from predators both in the air and on the ground? Explain.

_____

_____

_____

_____

Name _____

Read the task. Then, follow the steps to complete the task.

Wheel-y Fun

Create a working model of a waterwheel.

Materials

small plastic cups	string
pencils or dowels	tape
scissors	water
small disposable foam plates	

Ask

What do you already know? What do you need to know to get started? Where can you find the information you need?

_____

_____

_____

Imagine

What are the possibilities? Come up with several different options.

_____

_____

_____

Plan

Choose an idea. Draw a model and label it. Consider making different models for each stage of construction or separate diagrams of more complex parts.

📝 Plan

What are your steps? Use your drawing to guide your plan. Number your steps and write clearly so that others can understand them.

_____

_____

_____

_____

🛠️ Create

Follow your plan to create your model. What worked? What didn't? What did you need to change as you went through your plan? Why?

_____

_____

_____

🔄 Improve

How could you improve your model? Do you need to start over, or can you redo a single part? If it works, can it work even better?

_____

_____

_____

💬 Communicate

How well did it work? Is the problem solved? Write a statement to describe how your model meets the guidelines of the task and why it is successful.

_____

_____

_____

☀️ Reflect

How did you design your waterwheel to "catch" the water?

_____

_____

_____

_____

Name _____

Read the task. Then, follow the steps to complete the task.

Melting Master

Find a way to prevent candy from melting under a lamp.

Materials

aluminum foil   paper plate
chocolate chips   paper towels
cotton balls   plastic wrap
lamp   timer
newspaper

Caution: Before beginning any food activity, ask families' permission and inquire about students' food allergies and religious or other food restrictions.

Ask

What do you already know? What do you need to know to get started? Where can you find the information you need?

_____

_____

_____

Imagine

What are the possibilities? Come up with several different options.

_____

_____

_____

Plan

Choose an idea. Draw a model and label it. Consider making different models for each stage of construction or separate diagrams of more complex parts.

📓 Plan

What are your steps? Use your drawing to guide your plan. Number your steps and write clearly so that others can understand them.

_____

_____

_____

_____

🛠 Create

Follow your plan to create your model. What worked? What didn't? What did you need to change as you went through your plan? Why?

_____

_____

_____

🔄 Improve

How could you improve your model? Do you need to start over, or can you redo a single part? If it works, can it work even better?

_____

_____

_____

💬 Communicate

How well did it work? Is the problem solved? Write a statement to describe how your model meets the guidelines of the task and why it is successful.

_____

_____

_____

☀ Reflect

Do you think some kinds of candy melt more easily than others? Explain.

_____

_____

_____

_____

Name _____

Read the task. Then, follow the steps to complete the task.

Ready, Set, Recycle!

Create an educational game or puzzle with recycled materials.

Materials

bottle caps	glue
brass fasteners	kid-friendly magazines
cardboard	markers
cereal boxes	scissors
used wrapping paper	dice (optional)

Ask

What do you already know? What do you need to know to get started? Where can you find the information you need?

_____

_____

_____

Imagine

What are the possibilities? Come up with several different options.

_____

_____

_____

Plan

Choose an idea. Draw a model and label it. Consider making different models for each stage of construction or separate diagrams of more complex parts.

Plan

What are your steps? Use your drawing to guide your plan. Number your steps and write clearly so that others can understand them.

_____

_____

_____

Create

Follow your plan to create your model. What worked? What didn't? What did you need to change as you went through your plan? Why?

_____

_____

_____

Improve

How could you improve your model? Do you need to start over, or can you redo a single part? If it works, can it work even better?

_____

_____

_____

Communicate

How well did it work? Is the problem solved? Write a statement to describe how your model meets the guidelines of the task and why it is successful.

_____

_____

_____

Reflect

What are the pros and cons of using recycled materials? Which point is most important?

_____

_____

_____

Name _____

Read the task. Then, follow the steps to complete the task.

Bending Bubbles

Design a bubble wand that creates a square-shaped bubble.

Materials

bucket or large container
bubble solution (or a
    mixture of water and
    dish soap)

clay or play dough
drinking straws
tape
plastic pipette

Ask

What do you already know? What do you need to know to get started? Where can you find the information you need?

_____

_____

Imagine

What are the possibilities? Come up with several different options.

_____

_____

Plan

Choose an idea. Draw a model and label it. Consider making different models for each stage of construction or separate diagrams of more complex parts.

📓 Plan

What are your steps? Use your drawing to guide your plan. Number your steps and write clearly so that others can understand them.

_____

_____

_____

_____

🛠 Create

Follow your plan to create your model. What worked? What didn't? What did you need to change as you went through your plan? Why?

_____

_____

_____

🔄 Improve

How could you improve your model? Do you need to start over, or can you redo a single part? If it works, can it work even better?

_____

_____

_____

💬 Communicate

How well did it work? Is the problem solved? Write a statement to describe how your model meets the guidelines of the task and why it is successful.

_____

_____

_____

☀ Reflect

How did your knowledge of geometry help you complete the task?

_____

_____

_____

_____

Name _____

Read the task. Then, follow the steps to complete the task.

A-maze-ing Plants

Design a plant maze to prove that plants grow toward light.

Materials

cardboard
light source, such as a
   window or lamp
scissors

seedling or bean sprout
shoe box
tape

Caution: Before beginning any nature activity, ask families' permission and inquire about students' plant and animal allergies. Remind students not to touch plants or animals during the activity.

Ask

What do you already know? What do you need to know to get started? Where can you find the information you need?

_____

_____

_____

Imagine

What are the possibilities? Come up with several different options.

_____

_____

_____

Plan

Choose an idea. Draw a model and label it. Consider making different models for each stage of construction or separate diagrams of more complex parts.

📓 Plan

What are your steps? Use your drawing to guide your plan. Number your steps and write clearly so that others can understand them.

_____

_____

_____

_____

🛠 Create

Follow your plan to create your model. What worked? What didn't? What did you need to change as you went through your plan? Why?

_____

_____

_____

🔄 Improve

How could you improve your model? Do you need to start over, or can you redo a single part? If it works, can it work even better?

_____

_____

_____

💬 Communicate

How well did it work? Is the problem solved? Write a statement to describe how your model meets the guidelines of the task and why it is successful.

_____

_____

_____

☀ Reflect

In a forest of tall trees, how do smaller trees compete for sunlight?

_____

_____

_____

_____

Name _____

Read the task. Then, follow the steps to complete the task.

Starry Show-and-Tell

Create a planetarium to show various constellations.

Materials

2 light sources, such as flashlights or lamps	paper or disposable foam bowl or cup
black construction paper	scissors
cardboard box	sharpened pencil
glue	tape

Ask

What do you already know? What do you need to know to get started? Where can you find the information you need?

_____

_____

_____

Imagine

What are the possibilities? Come up with several different options.

_____

_____

_____

Plan

Choose an idea. Draw a model and label it. Consider making different models for each stage of construction or separate diagrams of more complex parts.

📝 Plan

What are your steps? Use your drawing to guide your plan. Number your steps and write clearly so that others can understand them.

_____

_____

_____

🔧 Create

Follow your plan to create your model. What worked? What didn't? What did you need to change as you went through your plan? Why?

_____

_____

_____

🔄 Improve

How could you improve your model? Do you need to start over, or can you redo a single part? If it works, can it work even better?

_____

_____

_____

💬 Communicate

How well did it work? Is the problem solved? Write a statement to describe how your model meets the guidelines of the task and why it is successful.

_____

_____

_____

☀️ Reflect

Why can't we see the stars during the day?

_____

_____

_____

_____

Read the task. Then, follow the steps to complete the task.

Newsworthy Towers

Create the tallest tower you can that can support the weight of an eraser on the top.

Materials

newspapers   tape
rubber eraser

Ask

What do you already know? What do you need to know to get started? Where can you find the information you need?

_____

_____

_____

Imagine

What are the possibilities? Come up with several different options.

_____

_____

_____

Plan

Choose an idea. Draw a model and label it. Consider making different models for each stage of construction or separate diagrams of more complex parts.

✏️ Plan

What are your steps? Use your drawing to guide your plan. Number your steps and write clearly so that others can understand them.

_____

_____

_____

_____

🔧 Create

Follow your plan to create your model. What worked? What didn't? What did you need to change as you went through your plan? Why?

_____

_____

_____

🔄 Improve

How could you improve your model? Do you need to start over, or can you redo a single part? If it works, can it work even better?

_____

_____

_____

💬 Communicate

How well did it work? Is the problem solved? Write a statement to describe how your model meets the guidelines of the task and why it is successful.

_____

_____

_____

☀️ Reflect

What factors limited the height of your tower?

_____

_____

_____

_____

Name _____

Read the task. Then, follow the steps to complete the task.

Slick Cleanup

Find a way to remove an oil spill from water.

Materials

coffee filters   vegetable oil
cotton balls   water
dish soap   water container
newspaper   yarn
paper towels

Caution: Before beginning any food activity, ask families' permission and inquire about students' food allergies and religious or other food restrictions.

❓ Ask

What do you already know? What do you need to know to get started? Where can you find the information you need?

_____

_____

_____

💭 Imagine

What are the possibilities? Come up with several different options.

_____

_____

_____

📝 Plan

Choose an idea. Draw a model and label it. Consider making different models for each stage of construction or separate diagrams of more complex parts.

📝 Plan

What are your steps? Use your drawing to guide your plan. Number your steps and write clearly so that others can understand them.

_____

_____

_____

✂️ Create

Follow your plan to create your model. What worked? What didn't? What did you need to change as you went through your plan? Why?

_____

_____

_____

🔄 Improve

How could you improve your model? Do you need to start over, or can you redo a single part? If it works, can it work even better?

_____

_____

_____

💬 Communicate

How well did it work? Is the problem solved? Write a statement to describe how your model meets the guidelines of the task and why it is successful.

_____

_____

_____

☀️ Reflect

How might an oil spill and cleanup occur in real life?

_____

_____

_____

_____

Name _____

Read the task. Then, follow the steps to complete the task.

Super Seesaw: Simple Machines

Create a device that can balance two unevenly weighted objects. Your device should be adjustable, and the cups should rest on top of the ruler.

Materials

disposable foam or
    paper cups
a variety of objects to
    weigh, such as pennies,
    dice, and erasers

pencil
ruler
tape

Ask

What do you already know? What do you need to know to get started? Where can you find the information you need?

_____

_____

_____

Imagine

What are the possibilities? Come up with several different options.

_____

_____

_____

Plan

Choose an idea. Draw a model and label it. Consider making different models for each stage of construction or separate diagrams of more complex parts.

Plan

What are your steps? Use your drawing to guide your plan. Number your steps and write clearly so that others can understand them.

_____

_____

_____

_____

Create

Follow your plan to create your model. What worked? What didn't? What did you need to change as you went through your plan? Why?

_____

_____

_____

Improve

How could you improve your model? Do you need to start over, or can you redo a single part? If it works, can it work even better?

_____

_____

_____

Communicate

How well did it work? Is the problem solved? Write a statement to describe how your model meets the guidelines of the task and why it is successful.

_____

_____

_____

Reflect

What did you notice about the placement of the ruler on the base? How did it relate to the size of the object being weighed on each side?

_____

_____

_____

Name _____

Read the task. Then, follow the steps to complete the task.

No Bones about It

Design a creature with an internal skeletal system. Your creature should be able to stand on its own.

Materials

art supplies, such as
   markers, paint, and yarn
clay or play dough
cotton swabs

craft sticks
glue
pencils
plastic straws

Ask

What do you already know? What do you need to know to get started? Where can you find the information you need?

_____

_____

_____

Imagine

What are the possibilities? Come up with several different options.

_____

_____

_____

Plan

Choose an idea. Draw a model and label it. Consider making different models for each stage of construction or separate diagrams of more complex parts.

📝 Plan

What are your steps? Use your drawing to guide your plan. Number your steps and write clearly so that others can understand them.

_____

_____

_____

_____

⚒️ Create

Follow your plan to create your model. What worked? What didn't? What did you need to change as you went through your plan? Why?

_____

_____

_____

🔄 Improve

How could you improve your model? Do you need to start over, or can you redo a single part? If it works, can it work even better?

_____

_____

_____

💬 Communicate

How well did it work? Is the problem solved? Write a statement to describe how your model meets the guidelines of the task and why it is successful.

_____

_____

_____

☀️ Reflect

How is your creature's skeleton similar to and different from your own skeleton?

_____

_____

_____

_____

Name _____

Read the task. Then, follow the steps to complete the task.

Blown Away: Erosion

Find a way to show how moving water can cause erosion.

Materials

beaker	plastic bin or pan
newspaper to protect surface	sand soil
pebbles	water

Ask

What do you already know? What do you need to know to get started? Where can you find the information you need?

_____

_____

_____

Imagine

What are the possibilities? Come up with several different options.

_____

_____

_____

Plan

Choose an idea. Draw a model and label it. Consider making different models for each stage of construction or separate diagrams of more complex parts.

Plan

What are your steps? Use your drawing to guide your plan. Number your steps and write clearly so that others can understand them.

_____

_____

_____

Create

Follow your plan to create your model. What worked? What didn't? What did you need to change as you went through your plan? Why?

_____

_____

Improve

How could you improve your model? Do you need to start over, or can you redo a single part? If it works, can it work even better?

_____

_____

Communicate

How well did it work? Is the problem solved? Write a statement to describe how your model meets the guidelines of the task and why it is successful.

_____

_____

_____

Reflect

In nature, what kinds of things help prevent erosion?

_____

_____

_____

Name _____

Read the task. Then, follow the steps to complete the task.

Motoring

Use rubber band energy to create a self-propelled vehicle such as a car or boat.

Materials

a variety of rubber bands   plastic bottle caps
cardboard   scissors
craft sticks   tape
glue   thread spools
pencils or dowels

Ask

What do you already know? What do you need to know to get started? Where can you find the information you need?

_____

_____

_____

Imagine

What are the possibilities? Come up with several different options.

_____

_____

_____

Plan

Choose an idea. Draw a model and label it. Consider making different models for each stage of construction or separate diagrams of more complex parts.

Plan

What are your steps? Use your drawing to guide your plan. Number your steps and write clearly so that others can understand them.

_____

_____

_____

Create

Follow your plan to create your model. What worked? What didn't? What did you need to change as you went through your plan? Why?

_____

_____

_____

Improve

How could you improve your model? Do you need to start over, or can you redo a single part? If it works, can it work even better?

_____

_____

_____

Communicate

How well did it work? Is the problem solved? Write a statement to describe how your model meets the guidelines of the task and why it is successful.

_____

_____

_____

Reflect

How was the energy of the rubber band transformed into motion in your design?

_____

_____

_____

_____

 © Carson-Dellosa · CD-104854 · Applying the Standards: STEM

Name _____

Read the task. Then, follow the steps to complete the task.

Asteroid Architect

Create an "asteroid" that can make a crater 2 inches (5 cm) across in a pan of flour when dropped from a distance of 1 yard (1 m).

Materials

a variety of balls
aluminum foil
baking pan
flour

newspaper
ruler
tape
yardstick or meterstick

Caution: Before beginning any food activity, ask families' permission and inquire about students' food allergies and religious or other food restrictions.

Ask

What do you already know? What do you need to know to get started? Where can you find the information you need?

_____

_____

_____

Imagine

What are the possibilities? Come up with several different options.

_____

_____

_____

Plan

Choose an idea. Draw a model and label it. Consider making different models for each stage of construction or separate diagrams of more complex parts.

Plan

What are your steps? Use your drawing to guide your plan. Number your steps and write clearly so that others can understand them.

_____

_____

_____

Create

Follow your plan to create your model. What worked? What didn't? What did you need to change as you went through your plan? Why?

_____

_____

_____

Improve

How could you improve your model? Do you need to start over, or can you redo a single part? If it works, can it work even better?

_____

_____

_____

Communicate

How well did it work? Is the problem solved? Write a statement to describe how your model meets the guidelines of the task and why it is successful.

_____

_____

_____

Reflect

What did you notice about the craters made by different materials?

_____

_____

_____

_____

Name _____

Read the task. Then, follow the steps to complete the task.

Moving with Magnets

Create a maze that can be navigated using only a magnet.

Materials

box lid	scissors
cardboard	tape
craft sticks	washers
magnet	

Caution: Keep small magnets and small pieces containing magnets away from young children who might mistakenly or intentionally swallow them. Seek immediate medical attention if you suspect a child may have swallowed a magnet.

Ask

What do you already know? What do you need to know to get started? Where can you find the information you need?

_____

_____

_____

Imagine

What are the possibilities? Come up with several different options.

_____

_____

_____

Plan

Choose an idea. Draw a model and label it. Consider making different models for each stage of construction or separate diagrams of more complex parts.

✎ Plan

What are your steps? Use your drawing to guide your plan. Number your steps and write clearly so that others can understand them.

_____

_____

_____

_____

⚒ Create

Follow your plan to create your model. What worked? What didn't? What did you need to change as you went through your plan? Why?

_____

_____

_____

↻ Improve

How could you improve your model? Do you need to start over, or can you redo a single part? If it works, can it work even better?

_____

_____

_____

💬 Communicate

How well did it work? Is the problem solved? Write a statement to describe how your model meets the guidelines of the task and why it is successful.

_____

_____

_____

☀ Reflect

Do you think you could guide a washer out of a glass of water with a magnet? Explain. Then, test your prediction.

_____

_____

_____

Name _____

Read the task. Then, follow the steps to complete the task.

For the Birds

Design a birdhouse and nest to attract a specific type of bird.

Materials

art supplies, such as paint
   and markers
clay
cotton balls
craft sticks
dowels
dryer lint
fabric

glue
hay
scissors
small boxes, such as
   tissue boxes or milk
   cartons
tape
yarn

 Ask

What do you already know? What do you need to know to get started? Where can you find the information you need?

_____

_____

_____

 Imagine

What are the possibilities? Come up with several different options.

_____

_____

_____

Plan

Choose an idea. Draw a model and label it. Consider making different models for each stage of construction or separate diagrams of more complex parts.

📝 Plan

What are your steps? Use your drawing to guide your plan. Number your steps and write clearly so that others can understand them.

_____

_____

_____

_____

🔧 Create

Follow your plan to create your model. What worked? What didn't? What did you need to change as you went through your plan? Why?

_____

_____

_____

🔄 Improve

How could you improve your model? Do you need to start over, or can you redo a single part? If it works, can it work even better?

_____

_____

_____

💬 Communicate

How well did it work? Is the problem solved? Write a statement to describe how your model meets the guidelines of the task and why it is successful.

_____

_____

_____

☀ Reflect

Describe the features of the bird that helped you determine the features of your birdhouse and nest.

_____

_____

_____

_____

© Carson-Dellosa · CD-104854 · Applying the Standards: STEM

Name _____

Read the task. Then, follow the steps to complete the task.

Shades of Color

Find the best black writing utensil to use to make an outdoor sign.

Materials

a variety of black markers
  and pens
cups
paper towel, cut into
  strips

poster board
water
spray bottle

Ask

What do you already know? What do you need to know to get started? Where can you find the information you need?

_____

_____

_____

Imagine

What are the possibilities? Come up with several different options.

_____

_____

_____

Plan

Choose an idea. Draw a model and label it. Consider making different models for each stage of construction or separate diagrams of more complex parts.

📒 Plan

What are your steps? Use your drawing to guide your plan. Number your steps and write clearly so that others can understand them.

_____

_____

_____

_____

🛠️ Create

Follow your plan to create your model. What worked? What didn't? What did you need to change as you went through your plan? Why?

_____

_____

_____

🔄 Improve

How could you improve your model? Do you need to start over, or can you redo a single part? If it works, can it work even better?

_____

_____

_____

💬 Communicate

How well did it work? Is the problem solved? Write a statement to describe how your model meets the guidelines of the task and why it is successful.

_____

_____

_____

☀️ Reflect

Think about why you did not use certain markers. What else did you discover about some markers?

_____

_____

_____

Name _____

Read the task. Then, follow the steps to complete the task.

The Floating Carrot: Density

Find a way to get a carrot to float on a water solution.

Materials

baby carrot   salt
flour   sugar
measuring spoons   water
plastic cup

Caution: Before beginning any food activity, ask families' permission and inquire about students' food allergies and religious or other food restrictions.

Ask

What do you already know? What do you need to know to get started? Where can you find the information you need?

_____

_____

_____

Imagine

What are the possibilities? Come up with several different options.

_____

_____

_____

Plan

Choose an idea. Draw a model and label it. Consider making different models for each stage of construction or separate diagrams of more complex parts.

📝 Plan

What are your steps? Use your drawing to guide your plan. Number your steps and write clearly so that others can understand them.

_____

_____

_____

_____

🔧 Create

Follow your plan to create your model. What worked? What didn't? What did you need to change as you went through your plan? Why?

_____

_____

_____

🔄 Improve

How could you improve your model? Do you need to start over, or can you redo a single part? If it works, can it work even better?

_____

_____

_____

💬 Communicate

How well did it work? Is the problem solved? Write a statement to describe how your model meets the guidelines of the task and why it is successful.

_____

_____

_____

☀️ Reflect

What might you conclude about how your solution is different than plain water?

_____

_____

_____

_____

Name _____

Read the task. Then, follow the steps to complete the task.

A Balanced Abode

Design a home for a "giant" that stays balanced on top of a paper towel tube "beanstalk."

Materials

art supplies, such as
  markers or crayons
cardboard
chenille stems
construction paper
cotton balls

craft sticks
glue
paper plate
paper towel tubes
scissors
tape

 Ask

What do you already know? What do you need to know to get started? Where can you find the information you need?

_____

_____

_____

Imagine

What are the possibilities? Come up with several different options.

_____

_____

_____

Plan

Choose an idea. Draw a model and label it. Consider making different models for each stage of construction or separate diagrams of more complex parts.

📝 Plan

What are your steps? Use your drawing to guide your plan. Number your steps and write clearly so that others can understand them.

_____

_____

_____

🛠 Create

Follow your plan to create your model. What worked? What didn't? What did you need to change as you went through your plan? Why?

_____

_____

_____

🔄 Improve

How could you improve your model? Do you need to start over, or can you redo a single part? If it works, can it work even better?

_____

_____

_____

💬 Communicate

How well did it work? Is the problem solved? Write a statement to describe how your model meets the guidelines of the task and why it is successful.

_____

_____

_____

☀ Reflect

Where is the balancing point of the giant's home you created? Can you add another item without affecting the balancing point?

_____

_____

_____

Name _____

Read the task. Then, follow the steps to complete the task.

Going Up!

Create a working elevator for an action figure.

Materials

action figure
empty thread spools
paper clip
pencil
scissors
small box

surface, such as a tall
    box, a stairway, or a
    table (to hang the
    pencil from)
tape
yarn or string

Ask

What do you already know? What do you need to know to get started? Where can you find the information you need?

_____

_____

_____

Imagine

What are the possibilities? Come up with several different options.

_____

_____

_____

Plan

Choose an idea. Draw a model and label it. Consider making different models for each stage of construction or separate diagrams of more complex parts.

📝 Plan

What are your steps? Use your drawing to guide your plan. Number your steps and write clearly so that others can understand them.

_____

_____

_____

🛠️ Create

Follow your plan to create your model. What worked? What didn't? What did you need to change as you went through your plan? Why?

_____

_____

_____

🔄 Improve

How could you improve your model? Do you need to start over, or can you redo a single part? If it works, can it work even better?

_____

_____

_____

💬 Communicate

How well did it work? Is the problem solved? Write a statement to describe how your model meets the guidelines of the task and why it is successful.

_____

_____

_____

✳️ Reflect

What else would your device work for?

_____

_____

_____

_____

Name _____

Read the task. Then, follow the steps to complete the task.

Cube-ism

Create a pattern for a paper cube on graph paper. Check to see if your pattern works by cutting it out and folding it into a cube.

Materials

graph paper   tape
pencil   ruler
scissors

Ask

What do you already know? What do you need to know to get started? Where can you find the information you need?

_____

_____

_____

Imagine

What are the possibilities? Come up with several different options.

_____

_____

_____

Plan

Choose an idea. Draw a model and label it. Consider making different models for each stage of construction or separate diagrams of more complex parts.

Plan

What are your steps? Use your drawing to guide your plan. Number your steps and write clearly so that others can understand them.

_____

_____

_____

_____

Create

Follow your plan to create your model. What worked? What didn't? What did you need to change as you went through your plan? Why?

_____

_____

_____

Improve

How could you improve your model? Do you need to start over, or can you redo a single part? If it works, can it work even better?

_____

_____

_____

Communicate

How well did it work? Is the problem solved? Write a statement to describe how your model meets the guidelines of the task and why it is successful.

_____

_____

_____

Reflect

What changes would be needed to make your cube larger?

_____

_____

_____

_____

Name _____

Read the task. Then, follow the steps to complete the task.

Banana Box

Create a lunch container that can open and close and that protects a banana from bruising.

Materials

Any items you choose, such as cardboard, chenille stems, and empty tissue boxes	banana glue scissors tape

Caution: Before beginning any food activity, ask families' permission and inquire about students' food allergies and religious or other food restrictions.

Ask

What do you already know? What do you need to know to get started? Where can you find the information you need?

_____

_____

_____

Imagine

What are the possibilities? Come up with several different options.

_____

_____

Plan

Choose an idea. Draw a model and label it. Consider making different models for each stage of construction or separate diagrams of more complex parts.

📝 Plan

What are your steps? Use your drawing to guide your plan. Number your steps and write clearly so that others can understand them.

_____

_____

_____

🪛 Create

Follow your plan to create your model. What worked? What didn't? What did you need to change as you went through your plan? Why?

_____

_____

_____

🔄 Improve

How could you improve your model? Do you need to start over, or can you redo a single part? If it works, can it work even better?

_____

_____

_____

💬 Communicate

How well did it work? Is the problem solved? Write a statement to describe how your model meets the guidelines of the task and why it is successful.

_____

_____

_____

☀️ Reflect

What other foods might your design be useful for? Would you need to change your design?

_____

_____

_____

Name _____

Read the task. Then, follow the steps to complete the task.

Reflection Collection

Create a light-and-reflection show for friends using mirrors.

Materials

mirrors   tape
flashlights

Ask

What do you already know? What do you need to know to get started? Where can you find the information you need?

_____

_____

_____

Imagine

What are the possibilities? Come up with several different options.

_____

_____

_____

Plan

Choose an idea. Draw a model and label it. Consider making different models for each stage of construction or separate diagrams of more complex parts.

✏️ Plan

What are your steps? Use your drawing to guide your plan. Number your steps and write clearly so that others can understand them.

_____

_____

_____

🛠️ Create

Follow your plan to create your model. What worked? What didn't? What did you need to change as you went through your plan? Why?

_____

_____

_____

🔄 Improve

How could you improve your model? Do you need to start over, or can you redo a single part? If it works, can it work even better?

_____

_____

_____

💬 Communicate

How well did it work? Is the problem solved? Write a statement to describe how your model meets the guidelines of the task and why it is successful.

_____

_____

_____

☀️ Reflect

What other materials might have been helpful for your show?

_____

_____

_____

_____

Read the task. Then, follow the steps to complete the task.

Sticky Situation

Create a glue that can make two pieces of paper stick together.

Materials

baking soda	paper
bowls	spoon
flour	sugar
measuring cups	water
measuring spoons	

Caution: Before beginning any food activity, ask families' permission and inquire about students' food allergies and religious or other food restrictions.

Ask

What do you already know? What do you need to know to get started? Where can you find the information you need?

_____

_____

_____

Imagine

What are the possibilities? Come up with several different options.

_____

_____

_____

Plan

Choose an idea. Draw a model and label it. Consider making different models for each stage of construction or separate diagrams of more complex parts.

Plan

What are your steps? Use your drawing to guide your plan. Number your steps and write clearly so that others can understand them.

_____

_____

_____

_____

Create

Follow your plan to create your model. What worked? What didn't? What did you need to change as you went through your plan? Why?

_____

_____

_____

Improve

How could you improve your model? Do you need to start over, or can you redo a single part? If it works, can it work even better?

_____

_____

_____

Communicate

How well did it work? Is the problem solved? Write a statement to describe how your model meets the guidelines of the task and why it is successful.

_____

_____

_____

Reflect

What materials do you think your glue will work best for? What materials do you think it will not work for?

_____

_____

_____

_____

Name _____

Read the task. Then, follow the steps to complete the task.

Making Music

Create a pan flute that plays eight different tones.

Materials

cardboard   straws
scissors   tape

 Ask

What do you already know? What do you need to know to get started? Where can you find the information you need?

_____

_____

_____

Imagine

What are the possibilities? Come up with several different options.

_____

_____

_____

Plan

Choose an idea. Draw a model and label it. Consider making different models for each stage of construction or separate diagrams of more complex parts.

Plan

What are your steps? Use your drawing to guide your plan. Number your steps and write clearly so that others can understand them.

_____

_____

_____

Create

Follow your plan to create your model. What worked? What didn't? What did you need to change as you went through your plan? Why?

_____

_____

_____

Improve

How could you improve your model? Do you need to start over, or can you redo a single part? If it works, can it work even better?

_____

_____

_____

Communicate

How well did it work? Is the problem solved? Write a statement to describe how your model meets the guidelines of the task and why it is successful.

_____

_____

_____

Reflect

What are some other instruments that play different tones in a similar way?

_____

_____

_____

_____

Name _____

Read the task. Then, follow the steps to complete the task.

Creating Creatures

Design and draw five new species of insects. Create an identification guide that includes the adaptations they have.

Materials

art supplies such as
   colored pencils,
   markers, or crayons

paper
stapler

Ask

What do you already know? What do you need to know to get started? Where can you find the information you need?

_____

_____

_____

Imagine

What are the possibilities? Come up with several different options.

_____

_____

_____

Plan

Choose an idea. Draw a model and label it. Consider making different models for each stage of construction or separate diagrams of more complex parts.

📓 Plan

What are your steps? Use your drawing to guide your plan. Number your steps and write clearly so that others can understand them.

_____

_____

_____

_____

🛠️ Create

Follow your plan to create your model. What worked? What didn't? What did you need to change as you went through your plan? Why?

_____

_____

_____

🔄 Improve

How could you improve your model? Do you need to start over, or can you redo a single part? If it works, can it work even better?

_____

_____

_____

💬 Communicate

How well did it work? Is the problem solved? Write a statement to describe how your model meets the guidelines of the task and why it is successful.

_____

_____

_____

☀️ Reflect

What features of your insects are like those of real insects?

_____

_____

_____

Name _____

Read the task. Then, follow the steps to complete the task.

Amusing Amusement Ride

Create a roller coaster that allows a marble to make a vertical loop.

Materials

cardboard tubes	marbles
chairs	scissors
glue	tape

Ask

What do you already know? What do you need to know to get started? Where can you find the information you need?

_____

_____

_____

Imagine

What are the possibilities? Come up with several different options.

_____

_____

_____

Plan

Choose an idea. Draw a model and label it. Consider making different models for each stage of construction or separate diagrams of more complex parts.

📝 Plan

What are your steps? Use your drawing to guide your plan. Number your steps and write clearly so that others can understand them.

_____

_____

_____

_____

🛠 Create

Follow your plan to create your model. What worked? What didn't? What did you need to change as you went through your plan? Why?

_____

_____

_____

🔄 Improve

How could you improve your model? Do you need to start over, or can you redo a single part? If it works, can it work even better?

_____

_____

_____

💬 Communicate

How well did it work? Is the problem solved? Write a statement to describe how your model meets the guidelines of the task and why it is successful.

_____

_____

_____

☀ Reflect

If you wanted your marble to make two vertical loops in a row, how would you need to change your roller coaster's design? Why?

_____

_____

_____

_____

 © Carson-Dellosa · CD-104854 · Applying the Standards: STEM

Name _____

Read the task. Then, follow the steps to complete the task.

Mapping Nature

Create a map and key of all of the natural things around your home.

Materials

binoculars
colored pencils
hand lens

pencil
plain paper or graph
paper

Caution: Before beginning any nature activity, ask families' permission and inquire about students' plant and animal allergies. Remind students not to touch plants or animals during the activity.

Ask

What do you already know? What do you need to know to get started? Where can you find the information you need?

_____

_____

_____

Imagine

What are the possibilities? Come up with several different options.

_____

_____

_____

Plan

Choose an idea. Draw a model and label it. Consider making different models for each stage of construction or separate diagrams of more complex parts.

📓 Plan

What are your steps? Use your drawing to guide your plan. Number your steps and write clearly so that others can understand them.

_____

_____

_____

_____

🛠 Create

Follow your plan to create your model. What worked? What didn't? What did you need to change as you went through your plan? Why?

_____

_____

_____

🔄 Improve

How could you improve your model? Do you need to start over, or can you redo a single part? If it works, can it work even better?

_____

_____

_____

💬 Communicate

How well did it work? Is the problem solved? Write a statement to describe how your model meets the guidelines of the task and why it is successful.

_____

_____

_____

☀ Reflect

Did you find more or fewer natural things around your home than expected? Explain.

_____

_____

_____

_____

Name _____

Read the task. Then, follow the steps to complete the task.

Playing with Playgrounds

Design a model of a playground with equipment that shows different properties of force and motion.

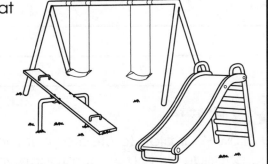

Materials

brass fasteners	scissors
cardboard	straws
cardboard tubes	string
chenille stems	tape
glue	craft sticks

 Ask

What do you already know? What do you need to know to get started? Where can you find the information you need?

_____

_____

_____

Imagine

What are the possibilities? Come up with several different options.

_____

_____

_____

Plan

Choose an idea. Draw a model and label it. Consider making different models for each stage of construction or separate diagrams of more complex parts.

📝 Plan

What are your steps? Use your drawing to guide your plan. Number your steps and write clearly so that others can understand them.

_____

_____

_____

_____

🔧 Create

Follow your plan to create your model. What worked? What didn't? What did you need to change as you went through your plan? Why?

_____

_____

_____

🔄 Improve

How could you improve your model? Do you need to start over, or can you redo a single part? If it works, can it work even better?

_____

_____

_____

💬 Communicate

How well did it work? Is the problem solved? Write a statement to describe how your model meets the guidelines of the task and why it is successful.

_____

_____

_____

☀️ Reflect

Which of your pieces of equipment relied on gravity to operate?

_____

_____

_____

_____